T0013337

WSkids
WHITE STAR KIDS

The Secret Lives of
Queens and Kings

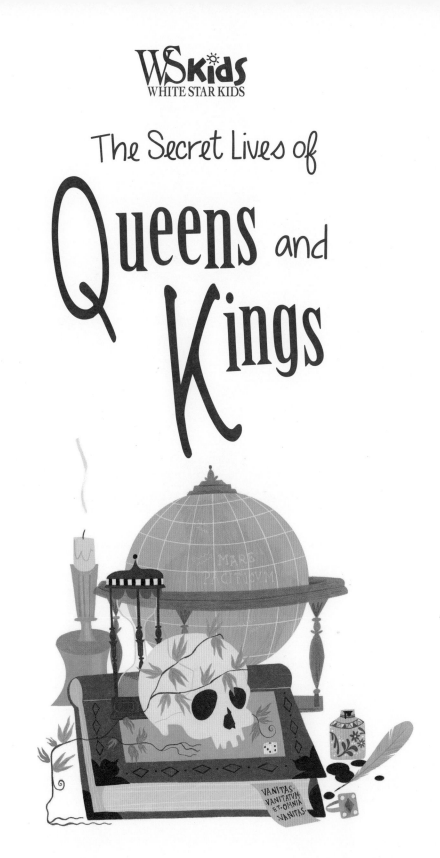

Illustrations by
LAURA BRENLLA

Text by
VERUSKA MOTTA

CONTENTS

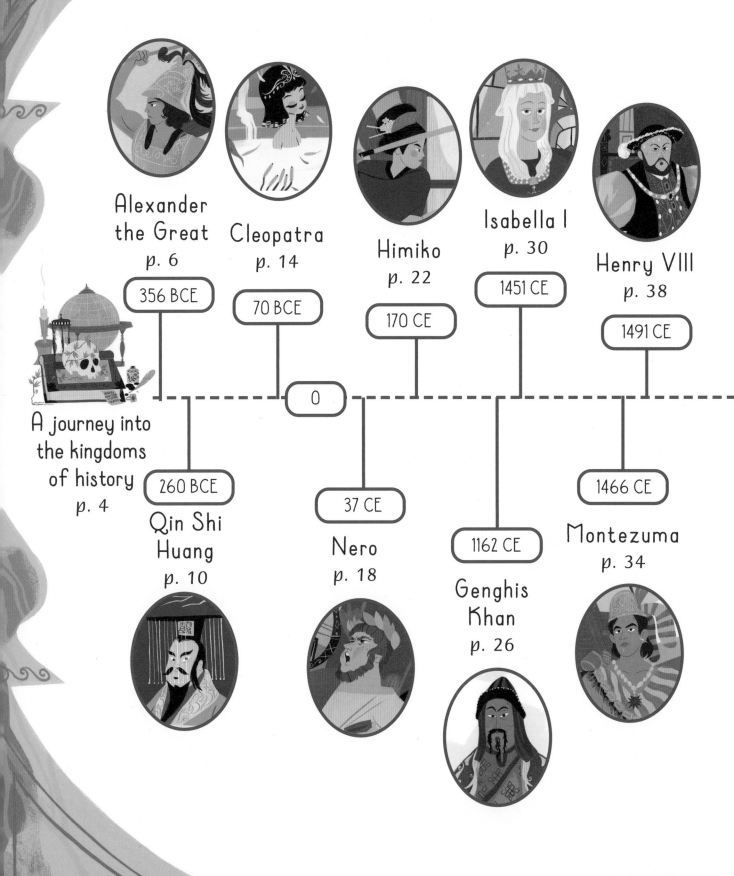

Alexander the Great p. 6

Cleopatra p. 14

Himiko p. 22

Isabella I p. 30

Henry VIII p. 38

356 BCE

70 BCE

170 CE

1451 CE

1491 CE

0

A journey into the kingdoms of history p. 4

260 BCE

37 CE

1162 CE

1466 CE

Qin Shi Huang p. 10

Nero p. 18

Genghis Khan p. 26

Montezuma p. 34

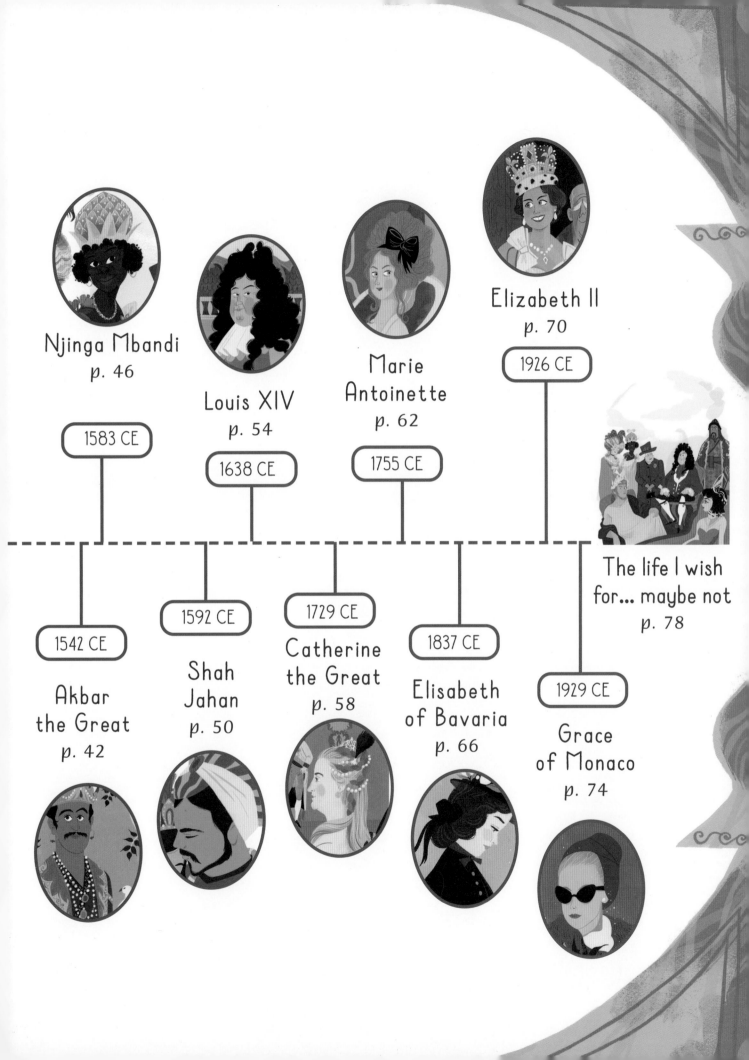

Njinga Mbandi
p. 46

1583 CE

Louis XIV
p. 54

1638 CE

Marie
Antoinette
p. 62

1755 CE

Elizabeth II
p. 70

1926 CE

The life I wish
for... maybe not
p. 78

1542 CE

Akbar
the Great
p. 42

1592 CE

Shah
Jahan
p. 50

1729 CE

Catherine
the Great
p. 58

1837 CE

Elisabeth
of Bavaria
p. 66

1929 CE

Grace
of Monaco
p. 74

A JOURNEY INTO THE KINGDOMS OF HISTORY

HAVE YOU EVER DREAMED OF LIVING IN A CASTLE?
Of wearing a crown and long robe encrusted with gleaming gems? Life at court looks wonderful: **PARTIES, BALLS, EPIC BATTLES, INTRIGUE,** and **VICTORIES.** Stories of royalty are often rich with action, surprising twists, journeys to faraway lands, incredible encounters...
Kings and queens have changed the lives of their subjects (perhaps not always for the better!), shaping the course of history forever.

They are often the protagonists of stories about their heroic gestures, their conquests, their beauty and wealth, their regal attitude, and their public appearances...but NOT ALL THAT GLITTERS IS GOLD (not even on a crown)! Away from the spotlight, betrayals, revenge, misdemeanors, obscure lives, bizarre palaces, and many other unusual facts lurk behind the scenes, and many could leave you speechless!

WOULD YOU LIKE TO DISCOVER THE SECRETS (AND WEIRD FACTS) OF SOME OF THE GREATEST MONARCHS IN HISTORY?

LET THE ADVENTURE BEGIN...

ALEXANDER III, KNOWN AS ALEXANDER THE GREAT
(356–323 BCE)

Three centuries before the birth of Christ, a king could enjoy the quiet life or could instead set off to conquer some nearby territory. "Why should I be happy with little?," Alexander III must have thought. Originally from Macedonia, this young king created the biggest empire of his time; from Greece to India, it covered an area of more than 3 MILLION SQUARE MILES. His actions were so grand that he was called "**Alexander the Great**"—not bad for someone who lived only 33 years!

He certainly wasn't the usual type. His teacher was **Aristotle**—one of the most important philosophers in history—and he obtained his first significant victory against the Greeks when he was just 18. He was a skilled warrior who loved risky challenges and aspired to extend his domain over all known lands. However, with great talent comes…GREAT DISCONTENT! He imposed many customs and traditions on the people that he conquered—even traditions from the **Persians**, who were bitter enemies of the Greeks and of many high officials in his army—and this led to general unrest, especially among the soldiers. After all, it was extremely difficult to keep everybody happy over such a vast empire!

He died suddenly, without an obvious cause. Was he sick? Was he poisoned by his officials? It is A TRUE MYSTERY that has not been solved to this day.

UNUSUAL FRIENDS

Even a king needs friends. Alexander knew he could count on his best friend, **Bucephalus.** They grew up together, facing adventures and battles of all kinds. A battle killed his friend, whom Alexander never abandoned until the last... NEIGH.

Yes, Bucephalus was a horse! Alexander organized a funeral for him with honors and dedicated an entire city to his memory (Alexandria Bucephalous, today called Jalalpur!).

AT YOUR BECK AND CALL...OR AT YOUR FEET?

Being called **"the Great"** doesn't help your modesty, and Alexander demanded his generals BOW DOWN AT HIS FEET, lying in front of him with their faces to the floor. It was a good position for a workout, but certainly not if you wanted to talk. With a couple of chairs, he could have avoided a lot of unhappiness!

OOPS, YOU SHOULDN'T HAVE SAID THAT!

"MOVE, LAZY!"

This might be something you say to friends who don't move from the sofa, but it isn't the right thing to say if you are talking to your soldiers, especially if they have been marching for 9,000 miles without a break (and fighting as well!). Alexander dreamed of conquering the world, while his army dreamed of a vacation!

A LITTLE REMINDER: IF YOU ARE IN CHARGE OF TROOPS, EVERY NOW AND THEN REMEMBER TO LET THEM STOP AND TAKE A NAP (AND MAYBE EAT A SNACK TOO)!

QIN SHI HUANG
(ca. 260–210 BCE)

Over 2,200 years ago, all the kingdoms of China were unified by the first Chinese emperor, who managed to do so in only 20 years. Rising to the throne when he was just 12 years old, Qin Shi Huang had a life full of mystery, but we have some evidence of his greatness (and of his weirdness!). Although he was just a boy, one of his first actions was to build an entire TERRACOTTA ARMY to guard...his TOMB! Over 8,000 soldiers, 130 chariots, and 670 horses can be seen today, but most of his immense necropolis is inaccessible because IT STILL LIES UNOPENED. Even if he was concerned with how to "furnish" the place where he would be buried one day, Qin Shi Huang did love life so much that he never wanted it to end. He made several journeys to find the **"mountain of immortality,"** and he sent his emissaries on reconnaissance. None of them managed to find the mountain, and as they feared being punished for this (Qin's fury was legendary), they all fled to Japan. Qin also demanded that the court doctors find a "cure for death"; they came up with some very special pills, but they certainly weren't what the emperor expected. The main ingredient in these pills was MERCURY, which at that time was believed to bring immortality, but today we know it to be a powerful POISON. And so, for a twist of fate, this elixir of eternal life ended up...KILLING HIM!

A SPACE WALL...
OR MAYBE NOT?!

Qin Shi Huang loved grand things. He wanted a wall built
to keep his enemies away and, of course, he wanted it big.
He ordered the construction of the **Great Wall of China**. It is one of
the Seven Wonders of the Modern World (even if the wall we see today
is largely a reconstruction), and it is almost 5,600 MILES LONG!
It has been said that it is the only human construction
visible from space, but astronauts have reported
that this is not true.

REFORMS THAT LEAVE THEIR MARK

If you think that the Chinese writing system is
difficult, you should know that it was even more so
before Qin Shi Huang's empire! He introduced one
unified writing system across the whole empire,
which was much "SIMPLER" than the previous
one. To make sure that everyone would
use it, he ordered all old books
to be burned.

OOPS, YOU SHOULDN'T HAVE SAID THAT!

"THIS IS JUST BETWEEN US"

In his mission to create a TERRACOTTA ARMY, the emperor hired over 700,000 people. It was a prestigious task, but the compensation for such hard work was...death! As he was afraid that those laborers would reveal the details of the work, Qin Shi Huang sent them to their deaths (some of them were actually buried alive!).

A LITTLE REMINDER: IT IS IMPORTANT TO ASK FRIENDS TO KEEP A SECRET, BUT IT'S BETTER NOT TO OVERDO IT WHEN IT COMES TO TAKING PRECAUTIONS!

CLEOPATRA
(70/69–30 BCE)

She has inspired poems, movies, comics, and cartoons characters. HOWEVER, HER REAL LIFE WAS MUCH GREATER THAN HER MYTH. The life of Cleopatra, the greatest queen of the ancient world, was truly exceptional. For instance, did you know that although she was the queen of the vast kingdom of Egypt, she was not Egyptian? She was ORIGINALLY FROM MACEDONIA, and her family spoke only GREEK. However, like a proper nerd, not only did she learn the language of her (future) people, but she also learned another six languages, along with studying science, mathematics, and dramatic arts. All these skills turned out to be very useful when she rose to the throne at 18 and started negotiating agreements with nearby territories, studying war strategies, and speaking personally to the inhabitants of her own kingdom.

She befriended the famous **Julius Caesar** and had an intense romance with an important Roman general, **Mark Antony**; she knew how to conquer lands... and warlords!

Such a special woman inevitably attracted a lot of gossip. Some said that her charm was the result of magical concoctions, whereas in reality it was simply coming from her great intelligence. When her enemies defeated her, she poisoned herself instead of surrendering to them.

SHE WAS VERY TOUGH
ALL THE WAY TO THE END!

OOPS, YOU SHOULDN'T HAVE SAID THAT!

"SHALL WE BET?"

During their honeymoon, **Cleopatra** and **Mark Antony** organized a "culinary" challenge to see who could set up the most expensive dinner. Sure of being the winner, Antony had a banquet set up, rich with extremely rare delicacies. However, Cleopatra took one of her pearl earrings, of immeasurable value, and had it melted inside a bowl filled with vinegar. She beat him with her wit, but in doing so she attracted the hostility of the Romans because they understood how smart she was.

A LITTLE REMINDER: A BET CAN BE FUN, BUT IT IS NOT NECESSARY TO WIN AT ALL COSTS!

FROM THE PYRAMIDS TO THE MOON

When we think about ancient Egypt, the pyramids immediately come to mind. However Cleopatra was born 2,500 years after the construction of the Great Pyramid... and "only" 2,029 years before man landed on the Moon!

NOSES UP

Cleopatra loved treating herself to moments of vanity; she would take long baths in donkey milk and would perfume herself with precious essences. We don't know exactly what she looked like, but we can guess...what HER SCENT WAS; during excavations, an ancient Egyptian perfumery was found and from that it was possible to recreate
THE FORMULA OF CLEOPATRA'S PERFUME!

NERO
(37–68 CE)

There are emperors who are much loved and others who provoke a deep hatred... and then there is Nero, who first conquered the Romans' hearts and later was forced to flee.

His accession to the throne was accompanied by a series of suspicious deaths, but the person responsible for his crowning was his power-hungry mother, **Agrippina.** One way or another, the boy with red hair and fair eyes (who was also a bit nearsighted) became emperor when he was only 16. By his side was **Seneca**, the most influential philosopher of the time, who taught him to love culture. The first years were perfect; even if his monarchy was absolute, his people loved him because he took away lots of privileges from the nobles. He organized great public events, games, and races that attracted the masses. He also gave money to the poor.

Nevertheless, it was not long before Nero started showing signs of madness. He thought everybody was antagonizing him, and he would do anything that sprang into his mind. Whoever tried to stop him ended up worse off, including his mother (what goes around, comes around!), his brother, and his old teacher. Even though the poor still loved their emperor, powerful people spread rumors against him until he was declared a "public enemy."

NERO WAS FORCED TO FLEE FROM ROME, AND HIS REIGN ENDED WHEN HE WAS ONLY 31.

TOO FIERY AN EMPEROR!

In 64 BCE a terrible fire spread throughout Rome for nine days and destroyed most of the city. Some thought that it was Nero who started it, even though others believed that he was away those days...but surely, the fact that he took advantage of the fire to have a new lavish palace built—the **Domus Area**—attracted a lot of suspicion to him.

WINNING IT EASY

Nero took part in the Olympic Games, beating the other contestants in the quadriga races (races with chariots drawn by horses).
WAS HE REALLY AN EXCEPTIONAL ATHLETE? Not really. He was definitely good, but the other athletes stopped when he flew off the chariot and then waited for him so that he could win, as they feared he would...fly off the handle!

OOPS, YOU SHOULDN'T HAVE SAID THAT!

"ARE YOU COMING TO SEE MY SHOW?"

Nero entertained himself with poetry, music, and theater, and his performances always had a large audience...because attendance was mandatory! Spectators were not allowed to leave the theater and had to show enthusiasm and appreciation if they wanted to avoid severe punishment.

A LITTLE REMINDER: IF YOUR FRIENDS REFUSE TO COME AND SEE YOUR DANCE OR MUSIC SHOW, DON'T HOLD A GRUDGE...APPRECIATE THEIR SINCERITY!

HIMIKO
(170–248 CE, dates are not certain)

In the remote past, over 20 centuries ago, the **Yamatai** kingdom was ruled by the gorgeous Himiko (the "**Daughter of the Sun**") who masterfully governed the vast area of modern-day Japan all alone.

According to stories passed down through generations, she obtained the crown thanks to her powers as a SHAMAN (a kind of priestess or sorceress). Whether this was true or not, she certainly was a special person; at that time women had very few rights and even fewer powers (and then only thanks to their husbands), whereas Himiko was not even married! She lived in a court that was inaccessible to the general public; 100 men would patrol its walls night and day, but they never came across the mysterious monarch. She was surrounded by 1,000 women attendants and only one man—A LOYAL ADVISOR (perhaps her brother) who would work as a link between her and the external world.

Her highest achievement was to bring PEACE and ORDER in a period of constant wars between conflicting regions. THIS WAS A TRUE PIECE OF MAGIC!

A SCREEN-FAMOUS EMPRESS

Do you know **Steel Jeeg**, the super-robot protagonist of Japanese manga cartoons and graphic novels? His biggest enemy is the queen of an ancient kingdom who has magical powers and an army of super-soldiers. Her name is **Himika...**

SOUNDS FAMILIAR, HUH?!

Traces of the mysterious empress can also be found in the **Tomb Raider** video game and films. In them, Himiko looks 2,000 years old and is represented as a terrifying mummy.

24

OOPS, YOU SHOULDN'T HAVE SAID THAT!

"WOULD YOU FOLLOW ME EVERYWHERE?"
Himiko's desire to be remembered in the afterlife was certainly understandable, but perhaps the 200 servants who were buried alive with her would have preferred a less epic end.

A LITTLE REMINDER: IT'S NICE TO HAVE YOUR DEAREST FRIENDS WITH YOU ALWAYS, BUT SOMETIMES IT'S MORE GENEROUS TO BE BRAVE AND CARRY ON ALONE!

A HOUSE FOR MEN ONLY

Even though the **Imperial House** was founded by Himiko, nowadays women are FORBIDDEN from becoming empresses in Japan. There were only about ten empresses in the whole history of Japan but Himiko isn't listed among them; her story is so full of mysteries that it wasn't included in the official list of the 125 emperors of the **Far East**.

GENGHIS KHAN
(1162/1167–1227 CE)

During the 13th century, a ruler of humble origins managed to unify a territory that spanned from Korea to the Balkans in only 25 YEARS (this territory was more vast than the Roman Empire, which had taken four centuries to be created!). Genghis Khan—one of the greatest conquerors of all times—had a LEGENDARY LIFE. He was expelled from his clan with his mother and his siblings, and he immediately learned how to survive by finding food and enduring the cold temperatures in winter. His youth is shrouded in MYSTERY; we know only that he became Great Khan—supreme ruler of the **Mongols**—thanks to the support of a powerful shaman.

Stories of him (such as the one about his father being a god!) are mixed with an incredible reality. He dreamed of becoming IMMORTAL, he wanted to conquer the world, and he was ruthless with his enemies (he would threaten them by saying "If you don't surrender, my soldiers will eat you alive!").

At the same time, he was FAIR WITH HIS SOLDIERS and was the finest warrior on horse; his "four-legged" army was notorious. After years of bloody conquests, he established the **Mongolian peace pax.** He united hundreds of different populations thanks to LAWS that were the same for all, one CURRENCY, a postal system, and a common WRITING SYSTEM.

At the moment just before his death—due to a hunting accident—he asked to be buried under an isolated tree. The vegetation grew all around him, COVERING HIS SECRETS FOREVER.

WHAT ARE THE STARS TELLING US?

Genghis Khan was always accompanied by **Yelü Chucai**, an excellent ASTROLOGIST, who looked up at the stars to tell the future, like a modern horoscope. The Khan consulted him before every expedition, a small **"superstition"** that brought many victories (actually, Yelü was also a great military strategist).

OOPS, YOU SHOULDN'T HAVE SAID THAT!
"WE'LL HAVE A SHOWER TOMORROW"

One of the characteristics of the Mongol army was...the SMELL! Genghis Khan encouraged his soldiers not to wash themselves; the horrible smell would be perceived from miles away and would help anticipate the arrival of the much-feared horde. It was a great tactic to scare people, but not so great for making new friends.

A LITTLE REMINDER: BEFORE MEETING NEW PEOPLE, IT'S BETTER TO WASH YOURSELF PROPERLY...YOU WOULDN'T WANT TO MAKE A "BARBARIC" IMPRESSION, RIGHT?!

LET'S HOPE IT RAINS!

At the time of Genghis Khan, exactly like today, CHANGES IN CLIMATE were very frequent; unusually heavy RAINS caused the Mongolian STEPPE to be covered with luscious grass that was perfect for feeding an army of horses! The great ruler thought of turning what was considered a simple means of transport into a true weapon that allowed thousands of soldiers to move fast and surprise their enemies.

ISABELLA I OF CASTILE
(1451–1504 CE)

Life at a European court in the 15th century was quite troubled-plagues, wars, attempted murder, rebellions, and many other dangers wouldn't let one sleep peacefully. Upon her brother Alphonso's death, Isabella of Castile became heir to the throne (which was held by her other brother, Henry IV), under the condition that she marry the king of Portugal. At 17, Isabella decided to follow her heart, rather than do what was expected of her, and secretly married her beloved, **Ferdinand of Aragon.** This led to the outbreak of WAR; for five years there were battles to decide who should govern. After Henry's death, Isabella ended up winning, and along with her husband, she immediately set off to conquer new territories. Not only did she invade with her army, but she also FORCED HER RELIGION upon her new subjects.

She was a tough woman, capable of untangling extremely complex political situations. She revealed herself to be forward-thinking when she sponsored a sailor who had already asked for money from the king of Portugal without success. Isabella gave him a lot of money (she even pawned her jewels) and THREE SHIPS. The mission was a success. As you may have guessed, the sailor was **Christopher Columbus,** and the mission resulted in the European discovery of America!

CONQUERING FREEDOM

When Isabella sponsored **Christopher Columbus**'s mission, she certainly couldn't have imagined that he would discover a whole new continent inhabited by a previously unknown population, the **Native Americans.** When she was informed that the native peoples were mistreated by the explorers, she got so angry that she had Columbus jailed (although not for long) and came up with laws that would make the relationship between colonizers and natives simpler and more humane.

EVEN QUEENS GO TO SCHOOL

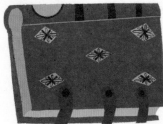

At that time, women were not allowed to study, not even at court, but Isabella knew very well that a queen in charge always needs to be one step ahead. She learned all the secrets of the CASTILIAN LANGUAGE (her own mother tongue), and she studied LATIN to be able to read books about military and political strategy. Thanks to her passion, she contributed tremendously to an increase in READING and PRINTING presses all over the country.

OOPS, YOU SHOULDN'T HAVE SAID THAT!

"READY FOR THE WEDDING?"

A woman who rebelled against conventions surely let her own children be free to choose whom to love, right? WRONG!

Isabella forced all five of her children into arranged marriages that helped her become even more powerful.

A LITTLE REMINDER: DON'T IMPOSE YOUR DECISIONS ON OTHERS. IT WILL CAUSE THEM TO TAKE YOU OFF THEIR "BEST FRIENDS" LIST!

MONTEZUMA
(ca. 1466–1520 CE)

Ruling one of the greatest civilizations in the Americas must not have been easy, but Montezuma did it quite well. At the end of the 15th century he was the emperor of the **Mexica people** (that's where the name "Mexico" comes from), today called the **Aztecs**. Their culture was rich, especially in science and myths; they believed that the world would end every 52 years, and they worshipped gods that resembled humans. Montezuma was more of a scholar than a warrior, but that doesn't mean that he gave up on bloody practices like many of his predecessors, such as HUMAN SACRIFICES!

During his reign, he increased the power of the capital Tenochtitlan, which was surrounded by water, like Venice, Italy (Mexico City was later built on its ruins). The end of his empire came at the hands of 500 Spanish conquerors, led by **Hernán Cortés**. Wrongly believed to be divine messengers, the conquerers were welcomed with honors by Montezuma, who gave them huge amounts of gold. It was a big mistake; within a couple of years, the greedy Spanish destroyed the entire Aztec civilization. However, the worst enemies of the last emperor were not armor and iron swords—which the Mexica people found to be strange and scary—but rather EUROPEAN DISEASES, which were unknown in the Americas and against which the population had no immune defenses.

SIGNS FROM THE SKY

Before the arrival of the Spanish, Montezuma had received signs announcing the END OF THE WORLD (the omen turned out to be true for his people). Among these signs was a COMET appearing in the middle of the day and a vision of MYSTERIOUS, MULTI-HEADED CREATURES. When the Mexica people saw the Europeans arrive on their horses, they actually thought that knight and horse were one creature!

A TERRIBLE REVENGE

After the emperor's death, the Spanish became ill from TROPICAL VIRUSES. They suffered from terrible stomachaches and had to go to the toilet all the time. That's how the legendary **"Montezuma's revenge"** was born—an illness that today still affects some travelers visiting Mexico and other areas of Central and South America.

OOPS, YOU SHOULDN'T HAVE SAID THAT!

"WOULD YOU LIKE A HOT CHOCOLATE?"

Cocoa is native to the tropical Americas and was unknown to Europeans. The first European to taste it was **Cortés**, who had been invited by Montezuma to drink a cup of CACAHUATL (hot chocolate) with him. To be precise, the conqueror's interest was actually in the cup, which was made of gold (although Cortés "stole" the cocoa, too, and took it back to Spain)!

A LITTLE REMINDER:

CHOOSE YOUR SNACK FRIENDS VERY CAREFULLY. IT WOULD BE A SHAME TO WASTE A GOOD CUP OF HOT CHOCOLATE (AND PERHAPS SOME COOKIES TOO) WITH SOMEONE WHO DOESN'T DESERVE IT!

HENRY VIII
(1491–1547 CE)

If **Shakespeare** himself—the most famous English playwright
and poet—dedicated an entire play to him, there must be a reason:
Henry VIII certainly wasn't like any other king, and he made English
and Irish history during the Renaissance by creating a powerful and
stable kingdom.

However, his choice of women was a bit erratic; within a period
of over 30 years he got married SIX TIMES...wedding organizers
at his court were surely never bored!
His handsome looks (at least in youth), his education (he spoke four
languages), and his power charmed women, but what moved Henry's
heart, more than love, were political alliances and his desire to have
a male heir. These "serial" marriages were, however, disliked by the
Catholic Church, which held great power in England at that time.
Henry didn't like being given orders, and so he DECIDED TO CREATE
HIS OWN CHURCH—the ANGLICAN CHURCH—and he appointed himself
as head of it.
This gave him even greater power, never again equaled in history,
without political or religious obstacles.

IT'S NO COINCIDENCE THAT HE WAS THE FIRST ENGLISH KING TO GIVE
HIMSELF THE TITLE OF "HIS MAJESTY" (AND SURELY NO ONE
DARED TO CONTRADICT HIM!).

HOT-HEADED...
OR HARD-HEADED?

A "**HEADER**" can be quite dangerous, as Henry found out. Among his adventures, he passed out after falling off his horse and plunging headfirst into a river! These types of ACCIDENTS were a hard blow to his pride and, most importantly, to his MEMORY; once he even forgot that he had locked his wife in the tower (and the poor lady had to wait a whole day in the cold to be let out). It's a shame that crash helmets hadn't been invented yet because they would have been useful to him!

OOPS, YOU SHOULDN'T HAVE SAID THAT!

"CAN WE HAVE AN ENCORE?"
Forget about the judges on cooking shows!
Henry VIII was much stricter than them
and demanded that only the best
recipes were served to him!
THE FACT THAT HE HAD A HEALTHY
APPETITE IS PROVEN BY HIS SIZE.

The king of England was a true
athlete when young, but he
became lazy through the years;
his waistline went from 31 to
51 inches (80 to 130 cm)!

A LITTLE REMINDER: A LITTLE
CANDY IS OK, BUT IT'S BETTER
NOT TO OVERINDULGE IF YOU
DON'T WANT TO CHANGE
YOUR SHAPE FROM "REGAL"
TO ROUND!

AKBAR THE GREAT
(1542–1605 CE)

Anyone who grows up during a war for the succession to a throne learns some important lessons, such as how to hunt and fight, but doesn't have much time left to learn to read or write. For this reason, Akbar, who rose to the **Moghul** throne when he was only 13, was ILLITERATE. However, he was a man of great culture (he had books of every kind read to him) and was revealed to be one of the most ENLIGHTENED emperors in history.

After UNIFYING THE VAST TERRITORIES of Afghanistan, Pakistan, and India, and being tired of religious wars, he allowed freedom of religion—A TRUE REVOLUTION!—and he even married a woman of a different faith than himself to show that peace was his priority.

The fusion of different cultures led to an extraordinary evolution in the ARTS and ARCHITECTURE. Akbar had great taste and really innovative ideas for the time. He created a proper artistic center that hundreds of people passed through and used to create breathtakingly beautiful works.

By merging the best of each population and each tradition, THE EMPEROR WAS SURELY FORWARD-THINKING! For this reason, Akbar truly deserved the name "**the Great.**"

SO BORING!

Akbar was a FINE INTELLECTUAL, but he could not stand long conversations. When he got bored, he would demonstrate this unapologetically with big YAWNS!

WILD PETS!

Among the emperor's many passions were ANIMALS: dogs, horses, camels, and pigeons, but mainly...ELEPHANTS! He would even organize elephant fights (let's just say that his garden looked very much like a jungle).

OOPS, YOU SHOULDN'T HAVE SAID THAT!

"I LIKE IT HERE!"

Akbar was also a skillful town planner. He chose to build his capital on a hill and called it **Fatehpur Sikri**, which means "**victory city**." It was a wonderful place, a cluster of elegant palaces, but it was abandoned after only 14 years because Akbar hadn't thought of a couple of details! The area was actually prone to DROUGHTS, and it wasn't very strategically positioned for when the emperor had to travel far away. It can be visited today—a hauntingly beautiful ghost town, left uninhabited for almost 400 years!

A LITTLE REMINDER: EVEN THE GREATEST IDEAS CAN TURN INTO BIG FAILURES. BEFORE STARTING AN AMBITIOUS PROJECT, DO YOUR RESEARCH AND GET ALL THE INFORMATION FOR YOUR VENTURE.

NJINGA MBANDI,
ALSO KNOWN AS
ANNA DE SOUZA
(1583–1663 CE)

In the 16th century, PORTUGUESE SLAVE TRADERS were quickly expanding all over the African continent. They certainly didn't imagine that they would be challenged by a woman, who would be a fierce, feared, and astute enemy. Her name was Njinga, the clever young daughter of the king of **Ndongo** (modern Angola). Her kingdom didn't start with the best of omens; when her father and her brother died, their enemies—the slave traders in particular—spread the rumor that it had been her fault. Moreover, her rise to power was not an obvious consequence of their deaths; as often happened, WOMEN WERE NOT PERMITTED TO RULE.

She reached her goal thanks to her cleverness. Aware that the best way to defeat an enemy is to know them, she STUDIED THE PORTUGUESE LANGUAGE AND CULTURE. She supported the slaves who had managed to escape, earning the TRUST OF HER PEOPLE, and married a head warrior so that she could have a loyal commander by her side.

She fought against colonialism and invasions of her country into her old age, but when she was 74, she signed a PEACE TREATY in order to concentrate on the needs of her people.

A DESTINY WITHIN A NAME

In Angola they say that Njinga was so named because she was born with her umbilical cord twisted around her neck (her name means "**twist**"). It was believed that a baby born this way was destined to have a WONDERFUL FUTURE as a leader. Definitely the right name then, huh?!

OOPS, YOU SHOULDN'T HAVE SAID THAT!

"WHERE CAN I SIT?"

During one negotiation, the Portuguese tried to humiliate Njinga by not even offering her a seat. She didn't let that discourage her; she called to one of her own slaves and she SAT ON HER BACK. This gesture proved her importance, even though the woman slave acting like a chair must not have been very enthusiastic about it.

A LITTLE REMINDER: WHEN FACING A CHALLENGE, FEEL FREE TO ASK YOUR FRIENDS TO GIVE YOU A HAND...BUT PERHAPS NOT THEIR BACK!

QUEEN OR WARRIOR?

When she was a young girl, Njinga clearly showed what a strong temper she had. She learned how to fight, wrestle, and use the WEAPONS of the time. When she was eight, her father allowed her to follow him, but not on a normal trip—he took her to war! Njinga grew with the SPIRIT OF A FIGHTER, even when faced with wars of DIPLOMACY.

SHAH JAHAN

(1592–1666 CE)

Being a child of the **Great Moghul** of India meant being prepared to fight for the throne. Prince **Khurram** knew that, and in order to rise to power, he had to defeat his own brothers, with imprisonments and violent deaths.

He managed to win and ruled under the name of Shah Jahan.

The **Moghul** Empire reached its peak under him; he transformed the army into a powerful weapon of war, conquering new territories and preventing ENEMY INVASIONS. He was also very passionate about architecture and had the most sumptuous palaces in India built for himself. Maybe as a kid, he would have enjoyed playing with Legos!

One of his most beautiful works of architecture came from a big loss: the DEATH of his beloved wife **Mumtaz Mahal**.

Because of the grief he suffered, Shah Jahan's BEARD turned WHITE. He then decided to build a **mausoleum** for her to be buried in, a breathtaking building to match the beauty of his wife. The result was the **Taj Mahal**, one of the Seven Wonders of the Modern World, a fairy-tale construction made of white marble, shells, and coral. IT REQUIRED 17 YEARS OF WORK BY 20,000 WORKERS AND MORE THAN 1,000 ELEPHANTS!

His reign ended in PRISON; his own son had apparently learned the lesson from his ancestors and had his father arrested in order to take power.

HAS ANYBODY SEEN THEM?

A legend says that Shah Jahan had all the people involved in the construction of the **Taj Mahal** disappear so that they could not build something that majestic ever again. Whether it's true or not, surely in the last 500 years no one has created something as extraordinary and BEAUTIFUL.

INDIAN NOTES

The emperor was a great lover of ARTS, and he especially enjoyed MUSIC. They say that his voice was celestial and everybody was enchanted when he sang. Perhaps he should have participated in *American Idol*?

OOPS, YOU SHOULDN'T HAVE SAID THAT!

"I'D LIKE TO EMBELLISH MY ROOM"

Once in power, Shah Jahan commissioned a special throne (the Peacock Throne) that featured PRECIOUS STONES worth millions of rupees (the Indian currency), and every year he would allocate enormous amounts of money to his JEWELRY collection, which was possibly the best in the world. He spared no expense, although his behavior nearly led his country to bankruptcy!

A LITTLE REMINDER: IF YOU DECIDE TO START COLLECTING SOMETHING, KEEP AN EYE ON YOUR WALLET.

LOUIS XIV OR THE SUN KING
(1638–1715 CE)

Being born within a royal court means attracting a lot of attention. Some would rather not have that, whereas others become famous precisely because they enjoy being the center of the world.

King Louis XIV of France was called the "**Sun King**"; everything had to rotate around him, like planets around a star. His motto was "I am the State" because he concentrated all powers in his hands alone. He deprived the aristocracy of any decision-making power and forced them to live with him in the vast palace at **Versailles**, a few miles from Paris, so that he could always keep an eye on them. He surrounded himself with art and beauty and hired the best artists of the time. His parties were legendary, with flamboyant costumes, special effects, and even fireworks. He spared no expense for his army, too, which in a few years increased from 65,000 to 400,000 soldiers. It was thanks to this immense military force that he transformed France into the greatest European power at the end of the 17th century.

A whole series of legends were created around him. One of the most famous ones is that of the **Iron Mask**, a mysterious prisoner with a mask on his face who was treated with the utmost respect.

WHO COULD HE HAVE BEEN? Maybe a spy who knew important secrets? Or maybe the king's twin? They are all fantasies that inspired copious literature on the character of this eccentric monarch.

OOPS, YOU SHOULDN'T HAVE SAID THAT!

"CAN I HAVE IT BIGGER?"

The Palace of Versailles was Louis XIV's dream, and he wanted to personally oversee its construction. However, perhaps he got carried away; every year he would request to make additions, and so the palace ended up with more than 700 rooms! It was the perfect building to celebrate the grandeur of the king, and it left everybody speechless...because of how much it cost.

A LITTLE REMINDER: IF YOU DECIDE TO START A NEW PROJECT, BE PRECISE WHEN TAKING THE MEASUREMENTS (AND MAKE SURE THAT YOU DON'T HAVE TO INVEST ALL YOUR FUTURE POCKET MONEY INTO IT!).

CAN I BE LEFT ALONE FOR A MOMENT?

Every single moment of his life, Louis XIV was followed by dozens of carefully selected servants, observers, and courtiers who would watch him wake up, get dressed, and eat. In case you are wondering...HE WAS EVEN FOLLOWED BY SOMEONE WHEN GOING TO THE BATHROOM (AND BEING PRESENT IN THOSE MOMENTS WAS CONSIDERED A GREAT HONOR)!

A TRUE ROYAL VEGETABLE PATCH

Parties, balls, luxurious clothes...however, Louis's true passion was GARDENING! He was taught by the head gardener how to prune plants and learned all the secrets of his favorite legumes, PEAS (this was one of the most popular topics of conversation at court!). He made sure that his vegetable garden contained the most precious vegetables, such as **eggplants**, which were very rare at the time; he even had 30 people tasked with polishing the eggplants before they could be served at his banquets!

CATHERINE THE GREAT
(1729–1796 CE)

The marriages of Russian tsars in the 18th century were rarely based on love, and that of young Princess Sophie was no exception. When she was 16, after changing her name to Catherine, she married **Peter III**, who was abusive toward her. She didn't get knocked down by that, though; she would repeat to herself that one is in charge of one's own happiness and misery. For this reason, she befriended many of the court soldiers, and when her husband became TSAR, she organized a coup and overthrew him with their help!

She had Peter arrested and forced him to sign a document stating that he abdicated the throne, leaving it to her.

Catherine II's kingdom was a true example of ENLIGHTENED ABSOLUTISM; she used her absolute power to help her people. She had studied the enlightened PHILOSOPHERS and believed that expanding access to education and improving the living conditions of her subjects were the foundations for Russia's development. She had HOSPITALS, PHARMACIES, and SCHOOLS (of medicine too) built all over the country, financing them by heavily taxing the richest people.

She was involved in many wars, but thanks to her diplomatic skills, she acted as a MEDIATOR between the monarchs of the great powers of Europe. She ruled for over 30 years, unifying all Russian territories; that is why she is remembered as the most powerful (and the last) TSARINA of history.

WHAT ARE YOU WEARING???

Catherine enjoyed dressing up as a man to go hunting and to lead her soldiers during parades, but her greatest passion was **costume parties**, which were very common at that time. Participants would swap roles, with men wearing embellished women's dresses and women dressing up in men's outfits.

OOPS, YOU SHOULDN'T HAVE SAID THAT!

"I WILL GIVE FREEDOM TO EVERYBODY"
During Catherine's time, millions of Russians were FEUDAL SERFS
who lived and worked as slaves for the landowners. Catherine began
declaring publicly that she wanted to give freedom to everybody
(or at least, to newborns).
Unfortunately, resources to allow such a vast reform were limited, and
the project was eventually abandoned, leaving everybody disappointed and
creating a lot of unrest. There was a RIOT and a violent attempt to rebel
against the tsarina, which was repressed by the army.

A LITTLE REMINDER: TRY TO MAKE PROMISES THAT YOU CAN KEEP
AND YOU WILL AVOID AN ANGRY CROWD (OR MAYBE EVEN JUST A
SMALL GROUP) WAITING OUTSIDE YOUR DOOR!

GAMBLING AT THE MUSEUM

The **Hermitage Museum** in
Saint Petersburg, Russia, is one
of the most visited museums
in the world today; it was built
by Catherine II to host her
private art collection, which
was open only to the court.
Sometimes she would go there
to play cards with her friends
(apparently, she lost a lot of
money on several occasions).

MARIE ANTOINETTE
(1755–1793 CE)

A beautiful woman, capable of conquering the hearts of nobles all over Europe, a lover of LUXURY and ENTERTAINMENT. That is how we remember Marie Antoinette, one of the most famous queens of France. However, her life was not exactly like that...AND IT WASN'T VERY MUCH FUN. When she joined the French court, Marie was only 15, a foreign girl (she came from Austria) away from her country and her family. She was there for political reasons, to marry the future king **Louis XVI**, who was 16 at the time. The two teenagers didn't even know each other and struggled to bond for many years. People at court scornfully called her **"the Austrian"** and circulated cruel rumors about her. Marie tried to forget about her sorrows BY SURROUNDING HERSELF WITH BEAUTIFUL THINGS.

She led a very unhappy life, although she was protected from her subjects, who were becoming angrier and angrier because of rising TAXES, WARS, and POVERTY. With the outbreak of the **French Revolution**, the king and the queen were SENTENCED TO DEATH. The angry mob was particularly cruel to Marie Antoinette. However, she faced her destiny with her head held high, and her fierceness was remembered even by the revolutionaries!

FAKE CAKE

Perhaps you've heard that tale that Marie Antoinette told the starving population, **"If they don't have bread, let them eat cake."** This is actually fake news; the sentence had been written in many books dating before her birth, but her ENEMIES spread this false rumor to make her reputation even more unpleasant!

A BEAUTIFUL SMILE

Before having Marie's official portrait made —which was the **painting** to be presented to her future husband—Marie's mother decided that her POSTURE had to be fixed, along with her TEETH. Following a visit with the most famous dentist of the time, Marie had to wear BRACES. They were very rudimentary, made of a piece of metal with lots of strings to pull, very similar to a TORTURE INSTRUMENT. But it worked! The future queen's smile was perfect!

OOPS, YOU SHOULDN'T HAVE SAID THAT!

"THIS PLACE IS NOT BAD!"
Marie Antoinette asked **Louis XVI** to give her
a palace near **Versailles**, the **Petit Trianon**, as
a present. It was a magical place, with a PARK
full of amusements, among which was an entire
village inspired by a PAINTING. Unfortunately,
the people, who were starving didn't appreciate
another royal treat.

A LITTLE REMINDER: INSTEAD OF BOASTING
ABOUT A BEAUTIFUL GIFT, IT'S BETTER TO SHARE
IT WITH OTHERS.

ELISABETH OF BAVARIA
(1837–1898 CE)

If she had been alive today, Elisabeth would have perhaps been a movie star or an Olympic athlete.

Her family was noble, but her mother was a bit unconventional and raised Elisabeth as a FREE SPIRIT, far from life at court, and taught her to take care of the poor.

However, Elisabeth fell in love with a man who came from a very different background: Emperor **Franz Joseph of Austria** (he was supposed to marry Elisabeth's older sister, but their hearts won).

The months of engagement were intense. Elisabeth hadn't studied much and now had to attend INTENSIVE COURSES, including IMPERIAL ETIQUETTE! After the wedding, it became clear that court life was not for her, with its strict rules and her interfering mother-in-law.

Elisabeth and Franz Joseph loved each other, but he was always away, and she was left alone among hostile people.

She rebelled against PALACE RULES many times, not just with tantrums but also with noble gestures, such as setting up a hospital inside the palace. People fought for the opportunity to see her because of her extraordinary beauty, not because they loved her. All over Europe RESENTMENT TOWARD ROYALS was on the rise. Elisabeth's life ended at the hands of a man who detested royalty (and who certainly didn't know that Elisabeth was critical of the court as well).

WHO ARE YOU?

Elisabeth of Bavaria is famously nicknamed **Princess Sissi**, but nobody called her that! In her family and at court she was known as LISI (or SISI, with one "s"), and she was a duchess and an empress, but NEVER a princess! This "wrong" name comes from a series of MOVIES about her life; directors took the liberty of changing the facts, and the name had such massive success that fiction overcame reality!

NEVER ONE HAIR OUT OF PLACE

Looking beautiful all the time was an OBSESSION for Elisabeth: washing her hair—which was so long it went to her ankles—took her SIX HOURS (and another TWO to style it every morning). After turning 30, she stopped allowing portraits of herself because she could not accept that she was ageing. She would never leave the palace without an UMBRELA or FAN, which she used to shield her face from PHOTOGRAPHERS (yes, paparazzi already existed!)

OOPS, YOU SHOULDN'T HAVE SAID THAT!

"SHALL WE GO FOR A WALK?"

Waking at 5:30 am, a cold shower, and three-hour workouts. This was not a SOLDIER'S TRAINING; it was Elisabeth's routine every morning.

And that's not all: She did hours of horseback riding, fencing, and long walks every day...her maids had to follow her although they would struggle to keep up!

A LITTLE REMINDER: SOME PHYSICAL EXERCISE IS GOOD FOR YOUR HEALTH, BUT DON'T OVERDO IT...OTHERWISE YOU'LL FIND YOURSELF ON YOUR OWN!

ELIZABETH II
(1926 CE–still reigning)

SHE IS THE LONGEST-REIGNING HEAD OF STATE IN THE WORLD, her particular way of waving at the crowds (which helps to avoid her arm getting too tired!) is often copied, and her bright outfits are covered in the pages of publications all over the world. We are talking about **Queen Elizabeth II of the United Kingdom** (Great Britain, Northen Ireland, and the Commonwealth).

There are many interesting facts about her life; in particular she was not expected to become queen. When she turned 10, her uncle, who was the king, decided to abdicate and leave the throne to his younger brother, **Lilibet**'s father.

From that moment on, her life was turned upside down with the immediacy of her "royal future." She never went to school and was instead educated by private tutors. She was the first monarch to send an e-mail (in 1976, between two military bases). She speaks "only" two languages—English, of course, and French, and her voice has reached the MOON, accompanying the astronauts of **Apollo 11**. She has been married for over 70 years to **Prince Philip**, and tabloids have always written about her and her family (often not too discreetly). Through it all, the most famous queen in the world continues to conquer people's hearts!

HAPPY BIRTHDAY TO YOU...
AND AGAIN...AND AGAIN

Although it is said you should never ask a lady her age, Elizabeth is proud to be over 90. Since she ascended to the throne, she has celebrated her birthday... MORE THAN 130 TIMES!

Traditionally, the British royals celebrate both on their date of birth (in her case it is the April 21) and on the SECOND SATURDAY OF JUNE, with a parade called **Trooping the Colour.** Does she receive twice as many presents?

YOUR ID, PLEASE?

Even though she has visited over 60% of the countries in the world (if you calculate the distance, it is like she has GONE AROUND THE WORLD 42 TIMES), Elizabeth has always traveled without ID! In the United Kingdom, passports and driving licenses are issued "in the name of the Queen," so she doesn't need to have either. Surely, she is one of those travelers who doesn't go unnoticed, but just to be sure, all her suitcases are personalized with the label **"The Queen."**

OOPS, YOU SHOULDN'T HAVE SAID THAT!

"I LOVE ANIMALS"

Everybody knows that the queen loves dogs (she has had over 300 **Corgis**) and horses (she started horseback riding when she was four). However, she has been given some very peculiar gifts because of her passion for animals, including an ELEPHANT, two GIANT TORTOISES, a JAGUAR, and two SLOTHS.

A LITTLE REMINDER: IF YOU ASK FOR A CUB AS A PRESENT (AND YOU COMMIT TO TAKING CARE OF IT), REMEMBER TO SPECIFY THE SIZE.

GRACE OF MONACO
(1929–1982 CE)

There have been MOVIES made in which a "regular" girl meets a prince through a peculiar set of events and ends up marrying him; this actually happened to Grace Kelly! When she started her career as an actress, she could never have guessed that her life would take such a twist. She was a real diva of breathtaking beauty and extraordinary talent; the most important directors of the time fought to have her in their movies.

It was on a movie set that she met her future husband, **Prince Rainier**, in 1955. That same year she fulfilled her biggest dream by winning an **Oscar**, the most important award in world cinema.

The following year she married Rainier, becoming the princess consort of MONACO, which is the second smallest country in the world (covering an area of only .78 sq miles, or 2 sq kilometers!). The princess turned it into one of the most glamorous and exclusive destinations in the world, loved by celebrities (many of who were her friends).

She had to give up her career as an actress, but she diverted her passion to organizing charity events and helping the less fortunate.

She unexpectedly died in a car accident, leaving behind the memory of an extraordinary woman and A FAIRY-TALE PRINCESS.

OOPS, YOU SHOULDN'T HAVE SAID THAT!

"LET'S STAY FRIENDS"

Thanks to her extraordinary beauty, Grace was always surrounded by admirers and amongst them, was another crowned head: Mohammad Reza Pahlavi, the last Shah of Persia, who tried to conquer her heart by giving her truly rare jewelry. However, as we know, Grace's destiny was to live in the Principality of Monaco, in the French Riviera.

A LITTLE REMINDER: DON'T GIVE IN TO POWER AND WEALTH, JUST FOLLOW YOUR HEART.

A ROYAL BARBECUE

Who says that princesses are always on a diet or eat only meals served by dozens of waiters? Grace Kelly loved American BARBECUES and would organize them at court—a true cooking revolution for the royal traditions!

DREAM OR NIGHTMARE WEDDING?

The whole world watched the royal wedding, which was THE FIRST TO BE BROADCAST ON LIVE TV. The wedding dress was made of more than 490 ft (150 meters) of fabric and almost 900 ft (300 meters) of lace. It certainly was a regal gown, but it wasn't easy to put on (and not lightweight either). The celebrations lasted TWO DAYS and were documented by 1,800 photographers.

SO STRESSFUL! Apparently, Grace sighed with relief when the last guest finally left.

THE LIFE I WISH FOR... MAYBE NOT

In over 2,000 years of history we have seen all sorts of things: greedy kings, queens obsessed with their physical defects (whether real or imaginary), and emperors who were easily tricked.

All these rulers have entered history thanks to either their MILITARY VICTORIES or the MAGNITUDE OF THEIR ACTIONS, but it is interesting, and exciting, to know that in reality they were more similar to us than what we have been led to believe. Instead of brave and legendary, some of them seem rather like ECCENTRIC characters, with BIZARRE, sometimes astonishing, behaviors.

If you've ever dreamed of a life at court, with dozens of servants always on call, fabulous balls, great adventures, and perhaps battles that require some heroic decisions, you now know that it actually isn't that easy! Days spent abiding by strict rules, boring obligations, enemies popping up everywhere, a marriage arranged by your family, relatives trying to steal your throne... NEVER A QUIET MOMENT FOR A MONARCH!

Have you ever thought that maybe kings and queens would dream to have a life...exactly like yours?!

VERUSKA MOTTA

An author and writer of books for children, Veruska is also an expert in communication and works in both capacities with several publishing houses. As an avid reader, she passionately alternates between books and comics.

LAURA BRENLLA

Laura started studying drawing when she was 16, although she grew up with a pencil in her hand. After winning a scholarship and graduating from the European University of the Creative Arts in Madrid, Spain, she attended a two-year course specializing in animation drawing. She was then selected for intensive training in digital cleanup at the prestigious animation studio SPA in Madrid, under the direction of Fernando Moro. It was here that she was able to deepen and hone her technical and artistic skills. Drawing has been her true passion ever since she held her first pencil. Recently she has illustrated several titles for White Star Kids.

Graphic layout:
VALENTINA FIGUS

WS White Star Kids® is a registered trademark property of White Star s.r.l.

© 2020, 2022 White Star s.r.l.
Piazzale Luigi Cadorna, 6
20123 Milan, Italy
www.whitestar.it

Revised Edition

Translation: Inga Sempel
Editing: Michele Suchomel-Casey

All rights reserved. No part of this publication may be reproduced, stored in a retrieval system or transmitted in any form or by any means, electronic, mechanical, photocopying, recording or otherwise, without written permission from the publisher

First printing, July 2022

ISBN 978-88-544-1875-2
1 2 3 4 5 6   26 25 24 23 22

Printed and manufactured in China by Guangzhou XY Printing Co., Ltd.